When Grandma Forgot My Name

by
Bernadeth Weekes

Gotham Books

30 N Gould St.
Ste. 20820, Sheridan, WY 82801
https://gothambooksinc.com/

Phone: 1 (307) 464-7800

© 2023 *Bernadeth Weekes*. All rights reserved.

No part of this book may be reproduced, stored in a retrieval system, or transmitted by any means without the written permission of the author.

Published by Gotham Books (December 16, 2023)

ISBN: 979-8-88775-481-9 (H)
ISBN: 979-8-88775-479-6 (P)
ISBN: 979-8-88775-480-2 (E)

Because of the dynamic nature of the Internet, any web addresses or links contained in this book may have changed since publication and may no longer be valid.

The views expressed in this work are solely those of the author and do not necessarily reflect the views of the publisher, and the publisher hereby disclaims any responsibility for them.

Acknowledgement:

Deepest gratitude to Susan Lakin, a loving grandmother, whose time spent with her grandchildren made it possible to create this book.

One day, my dad took my sister and me to visit our Grandma.
We were very happy to see our Grandma again.
We ran out of the car to hug her hello.

But when I ran up to her, she was different.
Grandma looked at me.

She said, "Little boy" and just kept looking at me.
I was looking up at her, but she could not say my name.
She looked confused and did not say my name.
Then, I said to Grandma, "It's me, Titus."
She said, "Oh! Titus."

I was six years old when my wonderful, loving Grandma could not remember my name.
I was confused and sad.
I could not understand what was happening to my loving Grandma.

My dad was surprised that she did not remember my name.
He told me that Grandma is ill and has trouble remembering a lot of things but that didn't mean that Grandma loves me any less.

I wrapped my arms around Grandma's legs. But she seemed uncomfortable and put her hands on my head. I was very sad.

We did not play with the multi-colored blocks on that day as we usually do.

After visiting Grandma in the
suburbs, I went to visit Oma,
my other grandmother.
I threw myself into her arms and cried.

Oma asked me what was wrong, and while sobbing, I said, "Grandma did not know my name."

Safe in her arms, I stayed silent as I cried.

I whispered, "Oma, I do not want you to get sick and not remember my name."
said, "I will be okay, sweetie. What did your dad say?" I replied, "My dad said that Grandma has an illness that makes her forget things, but she loves me and my sisters very much."

"That's right. Grandma loves you, but she's ill right now, and the illness causes her to forget a lot of things."
"Not only your name. She might not even remember your father."
Oma went on to explain the illness, she said:
"You see, sweetie, as we get older, some people suffer from an illness called dementia, which makes them forget important and little things."

22

Oma said that I should keep happy memories of Grandma in my mind and that I should focus on all the good times I had with her when she was well.
Oma then asked me to tell her about all the wonderful things I did with my grandma.
I started to reminisce and told Oma everything.

"When I was about 5, I remember visiting Grandma and she would lovingly put her hand on top of my head and say:
"I have to put a brick on your head because you are growing too fast."

"She would pick me up, I would put my arms around her neck, and we would laugh together."

"My Grandma lives in the suburbs, so I did not see her very often, but when my dad took my sister and me to visit her, it was always a happy day."

"When we visit, I remember my Grandma and me playing together with multi-colored building blocks in the living room."
It was always fun, and I loved playing with her.
This was our time together, and I was excited to see my Grandma.
One time, we built a tower that was taller than me with multi-colored blocks.

It did not start that way. It was just the usual short tower that we built, sitting on the floor in the living room.
Then, Grandma said that she had an idea. She got on her knees and continued building the tower. She asked me to hand the multi-colored blocks to her. She would name the color of the block she wanted, and I would give it to her.

When she finished the tower, it was taller than me.
My Grandma stood up and took me in her arms as we admired the tower.
"I remember this special time with Grandma and me playing with multi-colored blocks."

"My Grandma was a teacher but she can also do many different things.
I can remember sitting next to her while she played the piano.

She would play a tune, and then she would say to me, "Now, it is your turn to play!"
I just smiled and pressed the keys on the piano in front of me.
That was a very special time for me.
"I remember Grandma playing the piano with me."

"My Grandma loved flowers and had them growing in her garden. At the back of the house, there were a lot of stunning plants. I remember Grandma telling me about different plants and how to water them.

I remember Grandma teaching me how to water the plants. I still have the small watering can.
It was blue with a sunflower where the water came out.
It was so much fun."

"My Grandma loves sewing.
She was very good at making beautiful things.
She made a blankie with a sheep's head and my name on it.

It was my special blankie, and I took it everywhere I went.
I slept with my blankie.
She made blankies for all of us with our names on them.
I remember the blankie my Grandma made for me."

"Oh! Titus, you have so many wonderful memories of Grandma.
All these memories are full of the love you shared and the love she has for you.
I want you to always remember them.
So, when you see her next, remember them and know that she loves you, even if she forgets your name."

48

A couple of months later, Grandma could no longer live in her home.
She had to move into a special place that provided all the help she needed and kept her safe.
My dad and mom took us to see Grandma in her new home.
We took her out for a walk.
I held her hand while we walked outside of the building.
I was sad that she was ill, but now I never questioned her love for me.

My mind was filled with memories of the things we did together and her love for me.
The last time I saw my Grandma, she could not walk and was in a wheelchair.
I held her hand and she gently squeezed my fingers and looked at me warmly.
I did not know if she remembered me, and it did not matter.

Even if she can't remember the things we did together, I know my grandmother loves me.
I remember Grandma, and I love her so much.
Oma, I understand Grandma can't remember, but I do.
"My Grandma loves me."

www.ingramcontent.com/pod-product-compliance
Lightning Source LLC
LaVergne TN
LVHW070438070526
838199LV00036B/666